HOLY**HABITS** BIBLE REFLECTIONS | FELLOWSHIP

**The Bible Reading Fellowship**
15 The Chambers, Vineyard
Abingdon OX14 3FE
brf.org.uk

The Bible Reading Fellowship (BRF) is a Registered Charity (233280)

ISBN 978 0 85746 833 8
First published 2019
10 9 8 7 6 5 4 3 2 1 0
All rights reserved

Text © individual authors 2019
This edition © The Bible Reading Fellowship 2019
Original design by morsebrowndesign.co.uk & penguinboy.net

The authors assert the moral right to be identified as the authors
of this work

**Acknowledgements**

Scripture quotations marked NIV are taken from The Holy Bible, New
International Version (Anglicised edition) copyright © 1979, 1984, 2011 by
Biblica. Used by permission of Hodder & Stoughton Publishers, a Hachette
UK company. All rights reserved. 'NIV' is a registered trademark of Biblica.
UK trademark number 1448790.

Scripture quotations marked NRSV are taken from The New Revised
Standard Version of the Bible, Anglicised edition, copyright © 1989, 1995 by
the Division of Christian Education of the National Council of the Churches
of Christ in the United States of America. Used by permission. All rights
reserved.

Scripture quotations marked NLT are taken from the Holy Bible, New
Living Translation, copyright © 1996, 2004, 2007, 2013. Used by permission
of Tyndale House Publishers, Inc., Carol Stream, Illinois 60188. All rights
reserved.

Every effort has been made to trace and contact copyright owners for
material used in this resource. We apologise for any inadvertent omissions
or errors, and would ask those concerned to contact us so that full
acknowledgement can be made in the future.

A catalogue record for this book is available from the British Library

Printed and bound in the UK by Zenith Media NP4 0DQ

# FELLOWSHIP

## BIBLE REFLECTIONS
### 40 READINGS AND REFLECTIONS

Edited by
**ANDREW ROBERTS**

# Contents

# Contents

| Simon Reed

# Contents

Matthew Prior

## About the writers

**Nigel Wright** is a Baptist minister, theologian, author and former theological college principal. He comes from Manchester and lives in Cheshire.

**Helen Julian** CSF is an Anglican Franciscan sister and a priest, currently serving her community as Minister General. She has written three books for BRF and contributes to BRF's *New Daylight* Bible reading notes.

**Simon Reed** is an Anglican minister with two churches in Ealing, West London. He is also one of the three Guardians of the Community of Aidan and Hilda, an international and cross-denominational network of Christians who draw inspiration from Celtic spirituality for the renewal of today's church. He has written two books for BRF, *Creating Community* (2013) and *Followers of the Way* (2017).

**Matthew Prior** works on developing adult discipleship across the Diocese of Guildford, where he is also rooted in a local parish church. He has recently completed a doctorate exploring how Christians can make sense of living in increasingly technological societies.

## Introduction to Holy Habits

> They devoted themselves to the apostles' teaching and fellowship, to the breaking of bread and the prayers. Awe came upon everyone, because many wonders and signs were being done by the apostles. All who believed were together and had all things in common; they would sell their possessions and goods and distribute the proceeds to all, as any had need. Day by day, as they spent much time together in the temple, they broke bread at home and ate their food with glad and generous hearts, praising God and having the goodwill of all the people. And day by day the Lord added to their number those who were being saved.
>
> ACTS 2:42–47 (NRSV)

Holy Habits is a way of forming disciples that is emerging anew from an exploration of this precious portion of scripture, Luke's famous portrait of the early church. As such, it is both deeply biblical and an approach that lives when infused with the life-giving breath of the Holy Spirit – the same Holy Spirit who brought life, energy and creativity to the first Christian communities.

Holy Habits is based upon a series of ten practices that are shown to be fruitful in the Acts 2 passage: biblical teaching, fellowship, breaking bread, prayer, sharing resources, serving, eating together, gladness and generosity, worship, and making more disciples. In this series of material, passages relating to the ten habits are explored one habit at a time, sometimes with reference to other habits. In real life, the habits all get mixed up and complement each other as part of a holistic way of discipleship. You may want to be alert to such connections.

There are many lists in the Bible, and with biblical lists the first and last items often have particular significance. In this list, it is significant that biblical teaching comes first. All of the habits are to be found throughout scripture, and healthy holy habits will be grounded in regular engagement with biblical teaching. This is a foundational habit.

The last habit is also significant. Commentators have remarked that it is no surprise that 'day by day the Lord added to their number' when life was lived in the way Luke describes. Many can be nervous of the word 'evangelism'. Holy Habits offers a way of being evangelistic that may help to assuage some of those nerves.

Holy Habits is a way of life for followers of Jesus individually and collectively. In Acts 2:42–47, Luke offers clues as to how these practices can be fruitful. Note the devotion he mentions at the beginning and the repeated use of the word 'all'. Holy Habits is a way of life for all ages (including children), cultures and contexts. The habits are to be lived day by day, in the whole of life, Monday to Saturday as well as Sunday. And note how Luke attributes the growth that results to the Lord. These are *holy* habits, which flourish when the Lord is at the centre of all.

## Introduction to Fellowship

The Greek word translated as 'fellowship' in Acts 2 is *koinonia*. It is a word rich in depth, meaning and challenge. It points to a quality of relationship and activity which is much, much deeper than the chit-chat over a tepid cup of tea that is sadly often described as fellowship after many a Sunday service.

*Koinonia* is profoundly practical and deeply relational. John Stott argues that this *koinonia* 'is a Trinitarian experience, it is our common share in God, Father, Son and Holy Spirit. It also expresses what disciples of Jesus share together, what we give as well as what we receive' (*The Message of Acts*, Inter-Varsity Press, 1990). C.K. Barrett suggests that the fellowship was 'based upon common acceptance of the apostolic message [and] came into action in charitable use of its material resources' (*Acts 1—14*, T&T Clark, 2004). David Watson points out that '*koinonia* in the New Testament occurs more frequently in the context of the sharing of money or possessions than in any other' (*Discipleship*, Hodder and Stoughton, 1981). So true fellowship is both deeply spiritual and profoundly practical.

The *koinonia* in Acts 2 is seen in followers of Jesus eating, praying and sharing resources together. In short, sharing their lives with each other and the world around them, in a prophetic symbol of the kingdom of God; a powerful sign of a Spirit-filled way of life that stands against the sinfulness of selfishness; a wonder of hope, reconciliation and generosity; and a true community of belonging and service.

As such, this is a habit that not just the church but also a frighteningly broken and fractious world urgently needs to rediscover and experience. Most of the reflections in this booklet focus on the practice of fellowship within the church. This is a good place to start, but in your thinking allow the Spirit to help you imagine how the principles you learn about and practise within the

Christian community can be lived within the wider world too. What might your office or staff room or community centre look and feel like if it too embraced the way of life Luke describes in Acts 2:42–47? How might our political debates be conducted in a more wholesome (holy) way if the principles of sharing we see in the passages studied guided these debates? And how might our economies be ordered?

In recent years, there has been a healthy and timely rediscovery of the importance of community within movements such as Fresh Expressions and New Monasticism. Timely because, in a world that in some ways is more connected than ever, more people than ever are lonely. This epidemic of loneliness has been growing for many years. As you reflect on this precious holy habit of *koinonia*, think and pray how it can be a gift you can share with a lonely neighbour, the shy person at work or a person at the bus stop on a rainy day.

| Nigel Wright

# Welcoming the Lord

## Genesis 18:1–5

The Lord appeared to Abraham near the great trees of Mamre while he was sitting at the entrance to his tent in the heat of the day. Abraham looked up and saw three men standing nearby. When he saw them, he hurried from the entrance of his tent to meet them and bowed low to the ground. He said, 'If I have found favour in your eyes, my lord, do not pass your servant by. Let a little water be brought, and then you may all wash your feet and rest under this tree. Let me get you something to eat, so you can be refreshed and then go on your way – now that you have come to your servant.' 'Very well,' they answered, 'do as you say.'

(NIV)

| Nigel Wright

### Reflection

As Abraham is the one with whom the story of the people of God begins, the things that happened to him are bound to be formative for us. Already, God has spoken to Abraham in a vision that disclosed God's purpose for him. Now God comes again to draw Abraham into fellowship with God's own self, and he responds with hospitality centred around eating together.

Truth to tell, this is a mysterious event, but the opening verse makes it clear that it is a manifestation and act of God. The fact that in the wider narrative God is variously identified as the 'Lord', 'three men' and 'angels' is a puzzle, one in which some have traced an early anticipation of the divine Trinity. What is clear is that here God takes form in order to be present to Abraham, just as in later passages God appears in a variety of ways and supremely is made incarnate in Jesus the Son of God and Messiah. Hospitality was, and is, a sacred practice in the east, and by his unambiguous welcome Abraham reveals his own openness to God.

The God who took definitive form for us in Christ continues to invite our welcoming acceptance of God's presence through fellowship with the people of God, in the Spirit and in the spirit of Abraham. This is not an optional feature, but an essential dimension of the Christian life.

> Reflect upon your main sources of Christian fellowship,
> and be grateful.

| Nigel Wright

# Sharing the load

## Exodus 18:17–23 (abridged)

Moses' father-in-law replied, 'What you are doing is not good. You and these people who come to you will only wear yourselves out... You must be the people's representative before God and bring their disputes to him. Teach them his decrees and instructions, and show them the way they are to live and how they are to behave. But select capable men from all the people... and appoint them as officials over thousands, hundreds, fifties and tens. Let them serve as judges for the people... That will make your load lighter, because they will share it with you. If you do this and God so commands, you will be able to stand the strain, and all these people will go home satisfied.'                    (NIV)

## Reflection

This passage is among the various 'firsts' that we find recorded in the Bible. It is the first example of delegation, and as such it is often mentioned in leadership courses. When the work becomes overwhelming, it becomes necessary to share it, to let others come alongside to carry the burden of guiding the people or parcelling out responsibilities. This is a necessary aspect of fellowship, the showing of mutual care by carrying burdens together.

It could be objected that if followed precisely, Jethro's advice would leave us with a model of church that is like a pyramid, with relationships extending from on high to below, a 'command' structure. It might further be considered that in the Christian community, relationships are preferable when they are mutual, sharing responsibilities between each other horizontally rather than vertically and for a shared aim. But the essential insight remains the same: in the mission of God there is too much work for any one of us to do. If it is to be done, it must involve all of us. The extent to which it does is the measure of how much might be achieved for God's kingdom.

Fellowship is more than enjoying each other's company. It involves common ownership of work that is to be done. In common endeavour, there can be huge, productive and joyful satisfaction.

> Think about the term 'the common good' and how you contribute to it. Could you contribute more or, like Moses, do you need to do less for a while?

15

| Nigel Wright

# Covenant commitment

## Ruth 1:14–17 (abridged)

Then Orpah kissed her mother-in-law goodbye, but Ruth clung to her. 'Look,' said Naomi, 'your sister-in-law is going back to her people and her gods. Go back with her.' But Ruth replied, 'Don't urge me to leave you or to turn back from you. Where you go I will go, and where you stay I will stay. Your people will be my people and your God my God. Where you die I will die, and there I will be buried. May the Lord deal with me, be it ever so severely, if even death separates you and me.'　(NIV)

Nigel Wright

## Reflection

Belonging to God's people means being part of a covenant community. From our beginnings with Abraham, we have understood ourselves to be in a covenant, a committed and bonded relationship, with the God who has chosen us for a saving purpose. God has promised to be our God and that we will be God's own people. To be sure, this can be understood in a wrong way, as an assertion of superiority over others. Rightly viewed, it makes us servants of God's purposes, and so of the world.

Being in covenant with God carries with it the clear implication that we are also in a covenant relationship with each other, indeed with all who are counted as part of the fellowship of believers. We are bonded to each other and for God's sake are responsible for maintaining this bond of peace between us. Ruth was a Moabite rather than an Israelite, but she has the honour of a biblical book named after her, precisely because of the words we read here. She joined herself in faithfulness and loyalty to her mother-in-law, so embracing the God of Israel without reservation. In so doing, she earned a future and a hope and everlasting renown in the eyes of Israel.

The church is a covenant community. It is more than a convenience, a kind of service station on the motorway of life. It is a family, a community that shapes our identity, a divine initiative at the centre of God's purpose. It invites us to give it the kind of indissoluble commitment shown us by Ruth.

> How do you express covenant commitment in your local church and the universal church?

| Nigel Wright

# Reconstruction

## Ezra 3:1–2, 5–6

When the seventh month came and the Israelites had settled in their towns, the people assembled together as one in Jerusalem. Then Joshua son of Jozadak and his fellow priests and Zerubbabel son of Shealtiel and his associates began to build the altar of the God of Israel to sacrifice the burnt offerings on it, in accordance with what is written in the Law of Moses the man of God... They presented the regular burnt offerings, the New Moon sacrifices and the sacrifices for all the appointed sacred festivals of the Lord, as well as those brought as freewill offerings to the Lord. On the first day of the seventh month they began to offer burnt offerings to the Lord, though the foundation of the Lord's temple had not yet been laid. (NIV)

### Reflection

After years spent in exile in Babylon, the leaders of Israel and many others returned to Jerusalem and began to re-establish the shared life of the people of God. Note where they began and the principles they followed. At the heart of this spiritual renewal were the words of Moses as described in the Torah, the first five books of the Bible. Guided by this biblical teaching, they began once more to offer sacrifices to the Lord, both those prescribed for the rhythms of the temple and the personal, freewill offerings brought by individuals as part of their own devotional lives. This worship was continuous, costly and habitual. It demonstrated the priorities that governed their lives: God was to be honoured in their midst even before a stone of the restored temple had been laid. After all, the worship of Israel's God was what the temple was all about.

God's people have often needed to be reformed and renewed; the need exists still every day. At the heart of any renewing work, the same elements are to be found: the living out of biblical teaching and the sincere intention to put God first, to sanctify God's name through prayer and worship in the midst of the people. Our fellowship together is not mere human companionship, but is shot through with divine presence and with spiritual vitality.

> What do you see to be in need of renewal or reconstruction in the church or in the world? Call upon the name of the Lord so that God will be put first.

Nigel Wright

# Perseverance

## Nehemiah 2:17–20 (abridged)

Then I said to them, 'You see the trouble we are in: Jerusalem lies in ruins, and its gates have been burned with fire. Come, let us rebuild the wall of Jerusalem, and we will no longer be in disgrace.' I also told them about the gracious hand of my God on me and what the king had said to me. They replied, 'Let us start rebuilding.' So they began this good work. But when Sanballat the Horonite, Tobiah the Ammonite official and Geshem the Arab heard about it, they mocked and ridiculed us. 'What is this you are doing?' they asked. 'Are you rebelling against the king?' I answered them by saying, 'The God of heaven will give us success. We his servants will start rebuilding.'

(NIV)

| Nigel Wright

### Reflection

It may be a spiritual law that anything worth attempting for God will encounter difficulties. Persistence and perseverance are supreme and necessary virtues. Fortunately, Nehemiah possessed these in abundance as he was divinely commissioned to rebuild the walls of Jerusalem. The three opponents mentioned almost have the character of pantomime villains. The ridicule and mocking they employed (accompanied by their misrepresentations, betrayals and malicious letter-writing) sowed the seeds of the later hostility between Jews and Samaritans. But Nehemiah was not to be overcome.

When confronted by similar circumstances, where do we find reserves of resolve and energy? In the God of heaven, of course. But the reference here to God's servants is also significant. To have those around us who will strengthen our hand in God, who will literally embody God's support of us by their presence, is invaluable. Happy are we if we have such persons alongside us.

Like Ezra, Nehemiah was about the work of renewing the people of God and rebuilding the city of Jerusalem, where God had chosen to dwell. It was costly, demanding work, requiring outstanding qualities of leadership and endurance. It was also a work that involved motivating and mobilising a dispirited and discouraged population. Such struggles are not unknown in today's churches, in which we often feel that we are victims of 'multiple overwhelmings' in a changing and problematic culture. We need our Nehemiahs. Even more, we need each other.

> Whose hands do you need to strengthen in God? Who can strengthen yours? Thank God for those who do.

| Nigel Wright

# The passionate community

## Psalm 111:1–8

Praise the Lord. I will extol the Lord with all my heart in the council of the upright and in the assembly. Great are the works of the Lord; they are pondered by all who delight in them. Glorious and majestic are his deeds, and his righteousness endures forever. He has caused his wonders to be remembered; the Lord is gracious and compassionate. He provides food for those who fear him; he remembers his covenant forever. He has shown his people the power of his works, giving them the lands of other nations. The works of his hands are faithful and just; all his precepts are trustworthy. They are established forever and ever, enacted in faithfulness and uprightness.

(NIV)

| Nigel Wright

Reflection

Being a Christian involves holding certain convictions, about God, about God's works, about God's grace and righteousness and about God's ways. Such convictions, and others alongside them, provide the framework of imagination within which we seek to live good and upright lives: a life of holy habits. There are some who think that we can separate behaviour and belief, as though the former can operate without the latter. But this is surely mistaken: belief and behaviour influence one another; how we think forms how we live, and the other way around.

Most of us find that our convictions wax and wane. Sometimes we burn with assurance and at other times the fire burns low. Thankfully, Christian fellowship can shape and strengthen our faith and lives. This psalm speaks of the 'council of the upright' and the importance for us of the 'assembly', the believing community. Here, what we believe together can be remembered, rehearsed and celebrated in the company of others. We can be fed and nourished.

Sometimes Christian communities are dismissed as subcultures, with the implication that they might become ghettos. But the fact is that culture is simply a conglomeration of subcultures, and we all belong to at least one. These might be families, circles of friends, tribes, professions or trades. They are where we can be at home, sharing with those of like mind. They are good for us when at their heart is something wholesome, like trust in God.

Identify your various subcultures, and pray for each of them in turn.

| Nigel Wright

# The joyful community

## Psalm 133

> How good and pleasant it is when God's people live together in unity! It is like precious oil poured on the head, running down on the beard, running down on Aaron's beard, down on the collar of his robe. It is as if the dew of Hermon were falling on Mount Zion. For there the Lord bestows his blessing, life for evermore.
>
> (NIV)

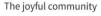

| Nigel Wright

This is a delightful psalm. Few things are more pleasing to God than heartfelt unity among those who belong to him. The church draws together the scattered and fractured people of the world into a new humanity in which barriers are abolished. In so far as we are alienated from each other, the human race has become a curse to itself and to creation. By contrast, when restored to a proper unity in Christ and the Spirit, we become fruitful and joyful; then we are at our best. For this reason, disunity among the churches is a matter of global concern.

The reference to 'pleasure' in the opening verse points to a neglected factor. Faith can become so serious in tone and so earnest in practice that we overlook the pleasure that the bonds of faith and spiritual experience bring with them. As the hymn says, 'Religion never was designed to make our pleasures less.' To be at one with others in the community of believers is a source of real joy. More than this, God bestows blessing where there is unity. One picture offered here is of the fragrant anointing oil being so abundant that, when poured on the high priest's head, it runs down to the collar. A second is of the life-giving dew of Mount Hermon falling on the people (Mount Zion) in ways refreshing and fruitful. Much to be desired.

Many of us have experienced the joy of kindred minds. There are challenges here: how to promote such unity, and how not to put any obstacles in its way. The psalm does not tell us how to meet these challenges; it is up to us to work it out.

First of all, desire such unity with a sincere heart. Then consider how you might enhance unity by living with gladness and generosity. Then pray for it.

Nigel Wright

# People

## Proverbs 27:6, 9–10, 13–14, 17

Wounds from a friend can be trusted, but an enemy multiplies kisses... Perfume and incense bring joy to the heart, and the pleasantness of a friend springs from their heartfelt advice. Do not forsake your friend or a friend of your family, and do not go to your relative's house when disaster strikes you – better a neighbour nearby than a relative far away... Take the garment of one who puts up security for a stranger; hold it in pledge if it is done for an outsider. If anyone loudly blesses their neighbour early in the morning, it will be taken as a curse... As iron sharpens iron, so one person sharpens another. (NIV)

### Reflection

Proverbs is a book of practical wisdom rather than doctrinal theology. It touches on a multitude of human experiences that all of us are able to identify with. These verses refer to some of the blessings and pitfalls of personal relationships, and by reflecting on them we might grow in wisdom about what to expect from people. Solidarity and fellowship with each other should be a basic commitment.

Friendship is among life's greatest delights, enriching each of us when it is a source of joy and pleasure. We need friends. Sometimes they are closer and more available to us than family members. For this reason, it is good to remain true to both friends and family, to be generous neighbours, to practise good will even when this might cost us. In a world becoming progressively less trusting and more suspicious, taking the risk of trusting others is a countercultural act.

Yet friends are not just there to make us feel good. They may wound us when, out of love, they speak the truth we do not like to hear. They may challenge our views so that we have to rework them in more satisfactory ways. Above all, these verses are an encouragement not to live selfishly but to be considerate (even to the point of not making antisocial noise!) and to promote harmony and concord to the best of our ability.

> Reflect upon who your neighbours are, geographically and socially. Take stock of your relationships and pray for them. Is there a friend you need to visit or call today?

Nigel Wright

# Life together

## Ecclesiastes 4:9–12

Two are better than one, because they have a good return for their labour: if either of them falls down, one can help the other up. But pity anyone who falls and has no one to help them up. Also, if two lie down together, they will keep warm. But how can one keep warm alone? Though one may be overpowered, two can defend themselves. A cord of three strands is not quickly broken. (NIV)

## Reflection

It has become evident that there is an epidemic of loneliness all around us. To be lonely is different from being alone. A person may choose to be alone and enjoy the experience, but to be lonely is to be bereft of human company in a way that threatens well-being. A moment's reflection indicates that it is impossible to become a complete human being without being nurtured through relationships that make healthy existence possible. Being well integrated in companionship with others brings abundant advantages, including, following these verses, warmth (sharing beds in a non-sexual way was common in former generations), mutual protection and assistance.

What is true of our existence is also true of work. There is something fundamentally cooperative about our life together. The great majority of us enjoy productive enterprises, working with others towards common goals and celebrating achievement. Through these we learn and grow, develop confidence and friendships and add to the quality of life. It is extraordinarily fulfilling to help meet the needs of other people.

Christians are called to be pastoral people (and the pastoral care of others is also a missional act). Inevitably, we will sometimes disagree with the ideologies and world views that others espouse, but this need not be a reason for showing lack of care. Rather, the opposite is true: because we need each other in the human family, we should go out of our way to transcend the barriers that divide us. In this way, we commend our faith. And it is within our Christian fellowships that we may learn the motivation and skills that enable pastoral care to ripple out from these communities into the world. If loneliness is on the rise, then Christians are supremely well placed to respond to it and to help towards its remedy.

What loneliness do you see around you? What are you in a position to do about it?

| Nigel Wright

# Visions of harmony

## Isaiah 11:6–9

> The wolf will live with the lamb, the leopard will lie down with the goat, the calf and the lion and the yearling together; and a little child will lead them. The cow will feed with the bear, their young will lie down together, and the lion will eat straw like the ox. The infant will play near the cobra's den, and the young child will put its hand into the viper's nest. They will neither harm nor destroy on all my holy mountain, for the earth will be filled with the knowledge of the Lord as the waters cover the sea. (NIV)

| Nigel Wright

This is a vision of the way things could be in God's good time – a direct reversal of our present condition in the world of nature and of human society. We are under threat. Conflict is common, almost endemic. The natural world is, in many places, in crisis. Why God has allowed it to be like this is one of the great mysteries; God has allowed the world to be and given it space to develop and grow within the limits given. Within this, and the freedom given to human beings in particular, we have a conflicted creation in which survival is paramount. We are part of this. Of course, this is not the whole picture – there is harmony and cooperation as well – but these verses are striking because they contrast so starkly with the way things are.

The good news is that things are set to change by way of divine gift. It is God's purpose to liberate creation from its various bondages and to bring it to liberty and healing, to put an end to the warring madness. It is an intriguing aspect of the vision that whereas the creatures mentioned remain what they are – wolves, leopards, cobras, lions – they cease and desist from their predatory and destructive ways. Likewise, in the new heavens and earth we will not cease to be human beings, but we will have ceased from sin and what goes with it.

In the meantime, the fellowship of God's people is called to be a sign and foretaste of what will be, of the promised future: a community that has ceased from doing harm.

> Pray for the peace of your church and community.
> With whom do you need to make peace?

# Reclaiming the lost

## Matthew 18:15–18

'If another member of the church sins against you, go and point out the fault when the two of you are alone. If the member listens to you, you have regained that one. But if you are not listened to, take one or two others along with you, so that every word may be confirmed by the evidence of two or three witnesses. If the member refuses to listen to them, tell it to the church; and if the offender refuses to listen even to the church, let such a one be to you as a Gentile and a tax-collector. Truly I tell you, whatever you bind on earth will be bound in heaven, and whatever you loose on earth will be loosed in heaven.'

(NRSV)

| Helen Julian

**Reflection**

This passage is the practical working out of the verses just before (18:12–14) about the shepherd going to find the lost sheep. It acknowledges that the church is not perfect, that its members still go astray and that it is in fact everyone's responsibility to act. The 'against you' in verse 15 may or may not be original – commentators' opinions vary. So this process applies whether the 'sin' is against a specific person or it entails more generally missing the mark expected within the community.

Notice what it doesn't say – the starting point is not telling everyone else how terrible someone is and how much they hurt me. Instead, the starting point is to take them aside quietly and speak to them, and, I'm sure, listen to them, as they perhaps explain what happened from their perspective. But if this doesn't work, then a few carefully chosen people should be brought in. And if that doesn't work, then the whole church (which here is the local community, not some larger body) needs to act.

It's very much a corporate process and responsibility; the power to legislate, to bind or to loose, is vested in the church as a whole, not just in its leadership. Throughout, it should be done in love and not in anger; the hope is to reclaim the 'lost sheep', not to drive it away. But it recognises also that there are real boundaries to fellowship, and sometimes people put themselves outside those boundaries.

How does your way of dealing with conflict measure up to Matthew's?

| Helen Julian

# Abiding in love

## John 15:1–5, 7

' I am the true vine, and my Father is the vine-
grower. He removes every branch in me that
bears no fruit. Every branch that bears fruit he
prunes to make it bear more fruit. You have
already been cleansed by the word that I have
spoken to you. Abide in me as I abide in you. Just
as the branch cannot bear fruit by itself unless
it abides in the vine, neither can you unless you
abide in me. I am the vine, you are the branches.
Those who abide in me and I in them bear
much fruit, because apart from me you can do
nothing... If you abide in me, and my words abide
in you, ask for whatever you wish, and it will be
done for you.'
(NRSV)

**Reflection**

When fellowship with other believers is proving difficult, we need to be reminded of its source. This much-loved passage is one of the most powerful reminders that it stems from the love and fellowship shared between the Father and the Son.

The context for these words of Jesus is the last supper, an intimate setting with his closest friends. But even they need to hear both that abiding is a choice and that God acts to cleanse and prune. Even after baptism, repentance and forgiveness continue to be needed, so that we become shoots which bear fruit. And bearing fruit does not primarily mean being successful, but following the pattern of Jesus' life. After all, how can healthy shoots be something other than the vine from which they spring?

It's easy for churches to become distracted by all the practical tasks – keeping the building in good condition, raising necessary funds, even seeking to bring in new members. But if the present members are not drawing sustenance from the vine, they will wither. It's easy to think that we just need to work harder, to put in more hours, in order for our fellowship to flourish. But if it isn't drawing on the relationship of Jesus and his Father, it will not bear fruit. Time for prayer, for quiet abiding, for reflection on scripture, is essential, and we need to encourage one another in these practices.

> Jesus, true vine, may I abide in you always, and so bear fruit and do your work.

| Helen Julian

# Grace for everyone

## Acts 2:1–6

When the day of Pentecost had come, they were all together in one place. And suddenly from heaven there came a sound like the rush of a violent wind, and it filled the entire house where they were sitting. Divided tongues, as of fire, appeared among them, and a tongue rested on each of them. All of them were filled with the Holy Spirit and began to speak in other languages, as the Spirit gave them ability. Now there were devout Jews from every nation under heaven living in Jerusalem. And at this sound the crowd gathered and was bewildered, because each one heard them speaking in the native language of each.

(NRSV)

### Reflection

It's like the reversal of Babel. In the Old Testament story (Genesis 11:1–9), people were scattered because they couldn't understand each other's speech; now, they are gathered together and everyone can hear and understand the good news.

Pentecost, also called the Feast of Weeks, was a harvest festival, and for Jerusalem it was the biggest pilgrimage of the year, bigger even than Passover. Pilgrims brought the first fruits of the wheat harvest, and for some it was also a time of covenant renewal. Now the disciples have just received the promised Holy Spirit, and the first fruits of this gift are words that everyone can understand. Not surprisingly, people are baffled – Peter has to explain what is going on and what it means for those gathered.

Every organisation has its own jargon – words which mean something to insiders, but which baffle outsiders. I sometimes listen to worship on the radio and wonder what an outsider would make of it: ordinary words with special meanings, words never used anywhere else. If we're to extend our fellowship beyond our own walls, we need to be very aware of the language we use. We can't make everything simple and instantly understandable – faith has depths which take a lifetime to understand. But we need to be willing, like Peter, to link what we say to our hearer's existing knowledge and experience.

Language can exclude or include; the gift of Pentecost is that God's grace is poured out on everyone, and our language as believers must reflect that.

> Consider how you would explain an important element of your faith to someone who doesn't yet believe.

| Helen Julian

# The work of transformation

## Romans 12:1–3

I appeal to you therefore, brothers and sisters, by the mercies of God, to present your bodies as a living sacrifice, holy and acceptable to God, which is your spiritual worship. Do not be conformed to this world, but be transformed by the renewing of your minds, so that you may discern what is the will of God – what is good and acceptable and perfect. For by the grace given to me I say to everyone among you not to think of yourself more highly than you ought to think, but to think with sober judgement, each according to the measure of faith that God has assigned. (NRSV)

### Reflection

This passage in Romans is the point where Paul turns from his theological teaching to its practical consequences. He has laid out justification by faith alone and expounded on life in Christ, and now he tells the Romans how they should live them out.

The key distinction is between conformity, to this world and its values, and transformation, to God's will and God's values. And this transformation will affect every part of us; we are to present our bodies and renew our minds. It is not just an emotional high or for a 'spiritual' portion of our lives. It is not just for Sunday or when we gather for worship. And perhaps this is one of the areas where we most need fellowship with one another, in order to keep on discerning 'what is good and acceptable and perfect'.

Transformation is not opposition; we don't live out this teaching simply by taking the opposite stand to anything which 'the world' values. We need to inform ourselves, exercise judgement and be open to admitting that we got it wrong and to changing how we think. Part of this will involve drawing on the gifts of the community of faith. Do you have scientists, teachers, carers, migrants or poets in your congregation? How can you use their knowledge and experience to inform your ongoing transformation? Thinking with 'sober judgement' is hard and sacrificial work, but it's necessary if we're to be the community which God calls us to be.

> Take an honest look at yourself. Can you identify one area of your life where you're too easily conformed to the values of the world around you? How could transformation happen there?

| Helen Julian

# With one voice

## Romans 15:1–7 (abridged)

We who are strong ought to put up with the failings of the weak, and not to please ourselves. Each of us must please our neighbour for the good purpose of building up the neighbour. For Christ did not please himself; but, as it is written, 'The insults of those who insult you have fallen on me.' For whatever was written in former days was written for our instruction... May the God of steadfastness and encouragement grant you to live in harmony with one another, in accordance with Christ Jesus, so that together you may with one voice glorify the God and Father of our Lord Jesus Christ. Welcome one another, therefore, just as Christ has welcomed you, for the glory of God. (NRSV)

### Reflection

Division in the church is one of the most off-putting sights for those outside it. If our fellowship with one another is marred by acrimony and bad feeling, why would anyone want to join us? But this passage has a deeper message than simply 'put up with one another'. To my ears 'putting up' comes with a sigh and the implication that I'm superior. The first verse here would be better translated as 'the strong must support the weaknesses of the weak'. This is a far more radical message.

Paul goes on to give three reasons for this practice: to build up the community; because this is what Christ did; and because the resulting strengthened body will be able to give God the glory and praise that he deserves.

One of the stark recognitions that has come with an increased focus on safeguarding is that we are all 'vulnerable' at times. The weak and the vulnerable are not 'them'; they are 'us'. We will all need support, if we don't already, because of sickness, bereavement, family troubles, mental health difficulties, etc. God's steadfast encouragement is for us to keep choosing the needs of others over our own, to support the weak rather than revel in our own strength. As we welcome one another, our harmony will glorify God in the eyes of others and draw them to ask why we do this.

> Reflect on what weaknesses in others you find most difficult to support at church, at work or at home. What one change might you make in how you behave?

| Helen Julian

# Disagreeing well

## Romans 16:17–19

> I urge you, brothers and sisters, to keep an eye on those who cause dissensions and offences, in opposition to the teaching that you have learned; avoid them. For such people do not serve our Lord Christ, but their own appetites, and by smooth talk and flattery they deceive the hearts of the simple-minded. For while your obedience is known to all, so that I rejoice over you, I want you to be wise in what is good, and guileless in what is evil.
>
> (NRSV)

### Reflection

I remember talking to a woman who was wondering about joining our community. 'It must be lovely,' she said, 'to be part of a group where everyone agrees.' 'It may be,' I replied, 'but this community isn't that group.' We may be united in our vocation, but we don't all think the same, from small issues (how to load the dishwasher) to large (how to relate to our neighbours of other faiths).

That isn't what Paul is warning against here. And it's a bit puzzling that he seems to be contradicting what he writes in the previous two chapters about not judging one another and bearing with the weak in faith. But when we look more closely, we can see that those were about problems within the community, whereas this warning is against those who, from outside, are seeking to teach a different doctrine.

Living well with one another doesn't mean never disagreeing; that can mean simply that those who have strong opinions always prevail, while others bite their tongues. The key is to find ways of disagreeing well, without causing dissension and offence. And that is hard; it means being willing to really listen to those with whom I disagree, to start from an assumption that their beliefs are genuine and founded in faith, as mine are. It means looking for what we have in common and where we can move towards one another.

And above all, it means seeking to serve Christ and not our own preferences. That is true wisdom and obedience and a witness to the world of a different way of relating.

> Reflect on how you deal with differences of opinion over what really matters to you. Are you willing to engage positively, or do you back off?

| Helen Julian

# Only Christ

## 1 Corinthians 1:10, 13–15, 17–18 (abridged)

Now I appeal to you, brothers and sisters, by the name of our Lord Jesus Christ, that all of you should be in agreement and that there should be no divisions among you, but that you should be united in the same mind and the same purpose... Has Christ been divided? Was Paul crucified for you?... I thank God that I baptised none of you except Crispus and Gaius, so that no one can say that you were baptised in my name... For Christ did not send me to baptise but to proclaim the gospel, and not with eloquent wisdom, so that the cross of Christ might not be emptied of its power. For the message about the cross is foolishness to those who are perishing, but to us who are being saved it is the power of God.

(NRSV)

### Reflection

One of the ways in which disagreement in the Christian community can become more entrenched is when leaders take up a particular position and gather around them only those who hold the same position. It becomes a matter of faith to agree with this person, and anyone who doesn't is marginalised or even forced out.

I'm unsure whether it's worrying or reassuring that this has obviously been a problem since the church began. Paul was perhaps seen as the 'superstar' among the wandering disciples; if you'd been baptised by him, you were somehow superior. It can be reflected today in the complaint that 'the church' hasn't visited a sick member, when what's really meant is that no matter how many church members have visited, the vicar or pastor hasn't – and that's who really counts.

Paul points, as ever, to what really matters – Christ and the power of his gospel. Anything else is secondary, leading us away from 'the same mind and the same purpose'. That doesn't necessarily mean that we will all think and act in exactly the same way; unity does not equal uniformity. But it does mean that we hold lightly to everything except the foolish message of the cross, which is a different kind of wisdom and a different kind of power.

Lord Jesus, may I cling only to you and to the power of your gospel, putting my faith in no one else.

| Helen Julian

# Only human?

## 1 Corinthians 3:1–6

And so, brothers and sisters, I could not speak to you as spiritual people, but rather as people of the flesh, as infants in Christ. I fed you with milk, not solid food, for you were not ready for solid food. Even now you are still not ready, for you are still of the flesh. For as long as there is jealousy and quarrelling among you, are you not of the flesh, and behaving according to human inclinations? For when one says, 'I belong to Paul', and another, 'I belong to Apollos', are you not merely human? What then is Apollos? What is Paul? Servants through whom you came to believe, as the Lord assigned to each. I planted, Apollos watered, but God gave the growth.

(NRSV)

## Reflection

We may not be flattered to be addressed as infants, but the reality is that the Christian life is one of lifelong learning – and the habit of fellowship is one that requires constant practice. Our normal human tendencies, which Paul refers to as 'the flesh', lead us away from the new way of life to which faith draws us, life as 'spiritual people'. It's easy to read into passages such as these a very negative attitude to the body, but this isn't what Paul means. For him, 'flesh' is much more about the inevitably flawed perspectives and motivations of our natural being. As we saw in the passage from Romans 12, we are called beyond that, to a transformation of our minds.

Jealousy and quarrelling are signs that this transformation is still to happen within a community and its members. These negative emotions spread an atmosphere that newcomers will pick up on, even if they don't experience them directly. Over the years, I've certainly visited churches and felt ill at ease, with no obvious cause. Later, I've learnt that people there were at odds with one another and that there were factions.

Once again, Paul directs his readers back to the centrality of Christ and to God's call to grow into his likeness.

> Reflect on your own spiritual journey. What has helped you to grow and to be ready for 'solid food'? Has this happened on your own or as part of a community of faith?

| Helen Julian

# One in Christ

## 1 Corinthians 12:12–13, 16–20 (abridged)

For just as the body is one and has many members, and all the members of the body, though many, are one body, so it is with Christ. For in the one Spirit we were all baptised into one body... If the ear were to say, 'Because I am not an eye, I do not belong to the body', that would not make it any less a part of the body. If the whole body were an eye, where would the hearing be? If the whole body were hearing, where would the sense of smell be? But as it is, God arranged the members in the body, each one of them, as he chose. If all were a single member, where would the body be? As it is, there are many members, yet one body. (NRSV)

## Reflection

If you've ever broken your ankle or suffered from sciatica, you'll know how every part of the body affects the whole. When one part is unable to function and contribute, everything else is thrown out of balance, having to work harder to compensate.

Paul has just written about the spiritual gifts. Now he goes on to write about the people who exercise these gifts – the members of the body of Christ. 'Body' is a startling picture for Paul to use. When he wrote, there would be people still alive who had seen the physical body of Jesus, before his death or after his resurrection. It's also a subversive picture. In Greek culture, it was normally used in a hierarchical way: the body worked well when everyone knew their place and kept to it. But here, every part is equally valued and equally necessary, and there is mutual dependence rather than hierarchy.

Churches traditionally tend to be hierarchical places, with some 'up the front' leading and others receiving what they give. But to be truly the body, all the gifts need to be fully used and equally valued. Some people will need help to value and express their own gifts; others, encouragement to step back and allow others to take the lead. God-given diversity is not a threat to unity and to fellowship; rather, it is what makes it possible and fruitful.

> What is your particular gift in the body?
> Are you using it fully?

| Helen Julian

# Love in practice

## 1 Corinthians 13:1–2, 4–8 (abridged)

> If I speak in the tongues of mortals and of angels, but do not have love, I am a noisy gong or a clanging cymbal. And if I have prophetic powers, and understand all mysteries and all knowledge, and if I have all faith, so as to remove mountains, but do not have love, I am nothing... Love is patient; love is kind; love is not envious or boastful or arrogant or rude. It does not insist on its own way; it is not irritable or resentful; it does not rejoice in wrongdoing, but rejoices in the truth. It bears all things, believes all things, hopes all things, endures all things. Love never ends. (NRSV)

## Reflection

If we could only have one passage to inform our reflection on fellowship, this would be it. It's often used at weddings, of course, and marriage is a particular form of fellowship. But the love that is essential to marriage is also the bedrock of all relationship, within the church and outside it.

The most wonderful spiritual gifts, if exercised without love, will count for nothing. Simply showing love and welcome can have a big impact. I served in a church which, by an accident of geography, had a very small congregation but a lot of weddings. Most of the couples had to worship with us for a time in order to be married there. And very ordinary members of the church, who wouldn't have seen themselves as having any particular gifts, had an impact by making them welcome, remembering their names and being glad to see them. It was love in action.

The negative behaviours that Paul names are ones of which the Corinthians themselves are guilty, so this teaching is quite personal and pointed. It's not a pink and fluffy picture of love, but an image of transformed behaviour, of love redefined by heavenly principles. It's Eliza Doolittle saying to Professor Higgins in *My Fair Lady*, 'Don't talk of love, show me.' And it is the one quality that 'never ends'. Other gifts and ministries might become impossible to exercise, but we can always show love.

> Which of the negative behaviours that Paul lists is your particular weakness? Be honest! How can you strengthen the positive exercise of love to overcome it?

| Simon Reed

# Reaffirm your love

## 2 Corinthians 2:5–11

If anyone has caused pain, he has caused it not to me, but to some extent – not to exaggerate it – to all of you. This punishment by the majority is enough for such a person; so now instead you should forgive and console him, so that he may not be overwhelmed by excessive sorrow. So I urge you to reaffirm your love for him. I wrote for this reason: to test you and to know whether you are obedient in everything. Anyone whom you forgive, I also forgive. What I have forgiven, if I have forgiven anything, has been for your sake in the presence of Christ. And we do this so that we may not be outwitted by Satan; for we are not ignorant of his designs.

(NRSV)

## Reflection

Don't ever assume that the New Testament church was a bed of roses. If the Christians at Corinth hadn't had so many problems, many of them about how to live in harmonious fellowship with one another, we wouldn't have two of Paul's longest letters. We don't know exactly what had gone wrong this time, but someone had done something that had caused offence to the church and to Paul. The problem was not ignored. It's likely that the punishment was exclusion from the fellowship meal where bread and wine were shared in memory of Jesus. It was a powerful way of saying that if you don't act like part of the body of Christ, you can't take part as a full member. How about your church? Do problems in relationships get addressed directly or glossed over?

But the most important thing is what happens next. Once the point has been made, forgiveness follows. Paul is emphatic that this must be just as strong as the action that was taken. The offender isn't just reinstated but has the love of everyone reaffirmed to them. The wound they caused must be loved back into wholeness to avoid evil infecting the whole body.

> Are you allowing an offence to fester? Have you spoken to the person who upset you? What can you do to reaffirm love for someone? Ask God's Spirit to help you, then do it.

| Simon Reed

# Agree with one another

## 2 Corinthians 13:11–13

Finally, brothers and sisters, farewell. Put things in order, listen to my appeal, agree with one another, live in peace; and the God of love and peace will be with you. Greet one another with a holy kiss. All the saints greet you. The grace of the Lord Jesus Christ, the love of God, and the communion of the Holy Spirit be with all of you.

(NRSV)

### Reflection

'Agree.' That would be easy if we all believed the same things about the Bible, worship, money, politics, sexuality, gender and the colour of the church carpet – and if some of us weren't so annoying. But Paul meant this and that's why he ends the most painful letter he had to write with his most famous prayer.

It's this prayer that makes agreement possible. Jesus is the embodiment of grace – total self-sacrifice on behalf of those who have done nothing to deserve it. That grace is the outflow of the God of love, who will give to the uttermost to save his creation, human and non-human. That grace and love are made present in our lives through the Holy Spirit, and because of this we are already in the deepest possible communion-partnership-fellowship-relationship there can ever be. Paul prays that this knowledge of God will be actively present with the divided and divisive Corinthians. If they can grasp afresh that this is what God is like, then they will be able to see that this is the way they are to think and act towards each other.

The radical truth is that what defines us as Christians is whether or not we have faith in this God. Everything else is of secondary importance. All the other things we argue about may be grounds for disagreement but never for dividing off from others. If we must disagree, we need to learn how to disagree well.

> What are the things which upset you most when other Christians think or act differently from you? Try to see those other people through the lens of grace, love and communion. Then pray for God to reveal these things to you afresh and work them out through what you say and do.

| Simon Reed

# Recognising grace

## Galatians 2:6–10

And from those who were supposed to be acknowledged leaders (what they actually were makes no difference to me; God shows no partiality) – those leaders contributed nothing to me. On the contrary, when they saw that I had been entrusted with the gospel for the uncircumcised, just as Peter had been entrusted with the gospel for the circumcised (for he who worked through Peter making him an apostle to the circumcised also worked through me in sending me to the Gentiles), and when James and Cephas and John, who were acknowledged pillars, recognised the grace that had been given to me, they gave to Barnabas and me the right hand of fellowship, agreeing that we should go to the Gentiles and they to the circumcised. They asked only one thing, that we remember the poor, which was actually what I was eager to do.

(NRSV)

## Reflection

Wherever Paul went, there was controversy. As a zealous Pharisee, he had no hesitation about using violence against Christians. As a new convert, he had difficulty being accepted as a genuine believer. As a missionary, he did not hesitate in drawing the radical conclusion that faith in Jesus meant that Gentiles did not need to follow the Jewish law. That led to friction with other, more conservative Jewish Christians. Although Paul was sure of his own calling, when he finally met the other apostles, he was not sure what reception he would get.

This was a huge issue. In the previous century, many martyrs had given up their lives rather than abandon the law. Nevertheless, James, Peter and John showed a discernment which enabled them to welcome Paul. They recognised God was at work in him just as God was in Peter, the other leading missionary, and they found a way for Christianity to be lived and to grow in two different but parallel ways, Jewish and Gentile. They grasped the essential truth that unity does not mean uniformity.

> How good are you at recognising where God is at work in people who are very different from you? Ask God to help you to listen to them and to him, and to be able to see his grace wherever it is.

| Simon Reed

# All of you are one in Christ

## Galatians 3:23–29

Now before faith came, we were imprisoned and guarded under the law until faith would be revealed. Therefore the law was our disciplinarian until Christ came, so that we might be justified by faith. But now that faith has come, we are no longer subject to a disciplinarian, for in Christ Jesus you are all children of God through faith. As many of you as were baptised into Christ have clothed yourselves with Christ. There is no longer Jew or Greek, there is no longer slave or free, there is no longer male and female; for all of you are one in Christ Jesus. And if you belong to Christ, then you are Abraham's offspring, heirs according to the promise.    (NRSV)

### Reflection

I don't like the Week of Prayer for Christian Unity! I dislike it for one simple reason: nowhere in the Bible are we told to pray *for* unity. Instead, as Paul does here, we are told that in Christ we *are* all one, and elsewhere (e.g. Ephesians 4:1–3) we're told to maintain that unity. Unity is expressed by actions. (And, just for the record, my church celebrates the Week of Prayer for Christian Unity with two other churches, where together we worship in four different languages.)

The biggest division in the early church was between Jewish and Gentile Christians, and in this letter Paul sets out why Greeks (non-Jews) don't have to keep the Jewish law, which by its very nature is all about being distinct from other peoples. That was radical enough, but these words also lay the foundations for the dismantling of an imperial system which took slavery for granted.

Think about the church or Christian group to which you belong. How much does it reflect racial, social and economic differences? Are men and women really treated equally? Would someone whose gender identity is non-binary feel comfortable in your gatherings?

> Spend some time silently picturing a church made up of the racial, social and gender diversity Paul describes here. Now ask the Holy Spirit to show you if there are any ways in which you don't treat people equally in your actions or attitudes. What might God want you to do differently? What about in places other than church?

Simon Reed

# Bear one another's burdens

## Galatians 6:1–6

My friends, if anyone is detected in a transgression, you who have received the Spirit should restore such a one in a spirit of gentleness. Take care that you yourselves are not tempted. Bear one another's burdens, and in this way you will fulfil the law of Christ. For if those who are nothing think they are something, they deceive themselves. All must test their own work; then that work, rather than their neighbour's work, will become a cause for pride. For all must carry their own loads. Those who are taught the word must share in all good things with their teacher.

(NRSV)

| Simon Reed

**Reflection**

Every church wants to think of itself as friendly. Many people love the idea of living in community, but as the 20th-century German martyr Dietrich Bonhoeffer pointed out, fellowship is about actions not ideas: 'The person who loves their dream of community will destroy community, but the person who loves those around them will create community' (*Life Together*, SCM Press, 1954).

Who do you know who is wandering off track in their Christian life? Is anyone getting alongside them? If not, what should you be doing? Who do you know in your church or group who is carrying a heavy load or facing a difficult situation in their life? What help do they need, and what can you do to provide it? Where are your church leaders struggling, and what could you do to help them more? Finally, are there times when we roll our eyes at someone else's mess rather than help them get out of it?

This is the down-to-earth, day-to-day stuff which makes or breaks fellowship. 'The law of Christ' is Paul's way of saying that we are called to act in self-giving love just like Jesus did.

> Spend a couple of minutes in silence, perhaps listening to your breathing to help you do that. Then go back to the list of questions above – you might be led to extend your thinking to colleagues or neighbours whose burdens you could share. Ask God to highlight for you the one which is most relevant. As a particular situation comes to mind, try to sense how God may be wanting you to respond.

# No longer strangers

## Ephesians 2:14–22

For [Christ] is our peace; in his flesh he has made both groups into one and has broken down the dividing wall, that is, the hostility between us. He has abolished the law with its commandments and ordinances, so that he might create in himself one new humanity in place of the two, thus making peace, and might reconcile both groups to God in one body through the cross, thus putting to death that hostility through it. So he came and proclaimed peace to you who were far off and peace to those who were near; for through him both of us have access in one Spirit to the Father. So then you are no longer strangers and aliens, but you are citizens with the saints and also members of the household of God, built upon the foundation of the apostles and prophets, with Christ Jesus himself as the cornerstone. In him the whole structure is joined together and grows into a holy temple in the Lord; in whom you also are built together spiritually into a dwelling-place for God.

(NRSV)

## Reflection

There's a lot of talk today about building walls to keep out people that some regard as unwelcome aliens. The biggest wall in ancient Israel was between Jews and non-Jews. The key elements of the Jewish law – food restrictions, male circumcision and sabbath-keeping – were designed to keep the Israelites separate from all other nations so that they did not lose their identity.

These, however, were only temporary measures, and Paul was one of the first to grasp that when Jesus the Messiah came, they were no longer necessary. God's worldwide people were now identified by the inner presence of the Spirit rather than by keeping laws. God's temple is no longer a building in Jerusalem – instead, God's special presence is wherever any of his people gather.

> Read that last sentence again a few times or, if you have time, reread the second half of today's passage. How does it shape how you think about yourself, the members of your group or church and the huge range of different churches and denominations? And how does it influence your thinking about walls (literal or metaphorical) that are being built between nations or different people groups at this time?

Simon Reed

# Grow up into Christ

## Ephesians 4:11–16

The gifts he gave were that some would be apostles, some prophets, some evangelists, some pastors and teachers, to equip the saints for the work of ministry, for building up the body of Christ, until all of us come to the unity of the faith and of the knowledge of the Son of God, to maturity, to the measure of the full stature of Christ. We must no longer be children, tossed to and fro and blown about by every wind of doctrine, by people's trickery, by their craftiness in deceitful scheming. But speaking the truth in love, we must grow up in every way into him who is the head, into Christ, from whom the whole body, joined and knitted together by every ligament with which it is equipped, as each part is working properly, promotes the body's growth in building itself up in love. (NRSV)

## Reflection

This chapter lifts to the highest level our ideas of what fellowship means. For all that it's nice to belong to a church where we feel genuinely welcomed and which meets our personal or family needs, God's vision for us and the body of Christ is so much bigger. God wants us to grow in our relationship with Christ and our imitation of Christ, and as that happens it also causes Christ's body, the church, to be built up and grow – which means nothing less than more and more people coming to faith.

This happens as all of us exercise our God-given gifts. The five mentioned here are often associated with church leadership roles, and therefore they are normally seen as only exercised by a relatively small number of people. Alan Hirsch, a cutting-edge mission theologian, argues persuasively that in fact all of us can share in these five gifts. Apostles are people who start things, prophets speak God's immediate word, evangelists bring others in, teachers show them how to be disciples and pastors build community.

> What role(s) do you have in your church or group? Reflect again on these five types of ministry. Which are you most drawn to? Ask God to work out this gifting more fully in your life.

| Simon Reed

# Be of one mind

## Philippians 2:1–8

If then there is any encouragement in Christ, any consolation from love, any sharing in the Spirit, any compassion and sympathy, make my joy complete: be of the same mind, having the same love, being in full accord and of one mind. Do nothing from selfish ambition or conceit, but in humility regard others as better than yourselves. Let each of you look not to your own interests, but to the interests of others. Let the same mind be in you that was in Christ Jesus, who, though he was in the form of God, did not regard equality with God as something to be exploited, but emptied himself, taking the form of a slave, being born in human likeness. And being found in human form, he humbled himself and became obedient to the point of death – even death on a cross. (NRSV)

**Reflection**

Does your church have a cross at the front? Do you break bread and drink wine together regularly? For most of us, the answer is yes. Do you also sometimes have sharp disagreements between people (maybe you've been part of one)? For many of us, the answer is also yes. Part of the reason is because we've lost sight of what the cross is all about. Jesus' death was not just a sacrifice on our behalf but also a pattern for how we are called to live.

Being of one mind does not mean we will always see things the same way. Looking to the interests of others sometimes means disagreeing with them. (I'm currently in a debate over one of the most controversial issues in the church today!) What Paul asks us to do is not to hide disagreement but, in it, to be like Jesus. Death by crucifixion is the ultimate and most visible loss of all power and status. Seeing relationships through the cross means recognising that we all needed Jesus to die for us and being willing to give up all attempts to control or coerce other people.

> 'I have been crucified with Christ; and it is no longer I who live, but it is Christ who lives in me' (Galatians 2:19–20). Sit with these words for a few minutes. What is God showing you?

# I want to know Christ

## Philippians 3:7–12

Yet whatever gains I had, these I have come to regard as loss because of Christ. More than that, I regard everything as loss because of the surpassing value of knowing Christ Jesus my Lord. For his sake I have suffered the loss of all things, and I regard them as rubbish, in order that I may gain Christ and be found in him, not having a righteousness of my own that comes from the law, but one that comes through faith in Christ, the righteousness from God based on faith. I want to know Christ and the power of his resurrection and the sharing of his sufferings by becoming like him in his death, if somehow I may attain the resurrection from the dead. Not that I have already obtained this or have already reached the goal; but I press on to make it my own, because Christ Jesus has made me his own.

(NRSV)

Simon Reed

### Reflection

Saul of Tarsus enjoyed ethnic purity among a people where that mattered. As a Pharisee, he belonged to a religious elite, and he was trusted by his country's ruling council. He gave all that up to follow Jesus, and his former friends became his active enemies. I know a person for whom conversion to Christianity from Islam means they have lost their job, are cut off from their family and cannot return to their country of origin. For people like that, belonging to a church means everything. They want to be there as often as possible. They want to help in any way they can.

To know Christ means more than deepening our personal relationship with him, important as that is. It's more than experiencing his resurrection power, important as that is. It also means sharing in suffering and experiencing loss. For some, that means undergoing persecution, but for all of us it means living a life of self-sacrifice – generosity, forgiveness, patience, listening, humility, compromise. Those values and practices are what build the deep fellowship-relationships we all ultimately seek and need.

> How much do you really want to know Christ right now? Be honest with God about your answer. Ask God to deepen your desire to be like Jesus and to inspire you to pursue that.

| Simon Reed

# Everyone mature in Christ

## Colossians 1:24–29

I am now rejoicing in my sufferings for your sake, and in my flesh I am completing what is lacking in Christ's afflictions for the sake of his body, that is, the church. I became its servant according to God's commission that was given to me for you, to make the word of God fully known, the mystery that has been hidden throughout the ages and generations but has now been revealed to his saints. To them God chose to make known how great among the Gentiles are the riches of the glory of this mystery, which is Christ in you, the hope of glory. It is he whom we proclaim, warning everyone and teaching everyone in all wisdom, so that we may present everyone mature in Christ. For this I toil and struggle with all the energy that he powerfully inspires within me.

(NRSV)

| Simon Reed

## Reflection

This passage contains one of the best definitions of what Christian life, mission and ministry is all about – enabling people to become 'mature in Christ'. My best explanation of that is that it's about connecting more deeply with God and connecting God with the whole of life. Because Christianity is irreducibly something we do together (notice how often Paul says 'we', and the 'you' also means 'all of you'), this also means connecting with other people.

The challenge we face is how to make deepening this threefold connection a lifelong intentional process. Many Christians are rediscovering the ancient (and arguably biblical) practice of working out a personal Way of Life – a short and simple set of commitments to help them stay on the path of following Christ and find their way back when they wander off. The ten holy habits are an example of this, and you can find other examples among the various new monastic communities which are springing up. The inevitable by-product of this intentional Christian living is that through us God will touch others.

> Take some time to reflect prayerfully on how the practice of fellowship is expressed in your life. What does your commitment to your church or Christian group look like? Are you clear about how you use your gifts to serve others? Is there anything you need to change?

| Matthew Prior

# The King's speech

## Colossians 3:12–16

Since God chose you to be the holy people he loves, you must clothe yourselves with tenderhearted mercy, kindness, humility, gentleness, and patience. Make allowance for each other's faults, and forgive anyone who offends you. Remember, the Lord forgave you, so you must forgive others. Above all, clothe yourselves with love, which binds us all together in perfect harmony. And let the peace that comes from Christ rule in your hearts. For as members of one body you are called to live in peace. And always be thankful. Let the message about Christ, in all its richness, fill your lives. Teach and counsel each other with all the wisdom he gives. Sing psalms and hymns and spiritual songs to God with thankful hearts. (NLT)

### Reflection

Theories of the origins of human language diverge widely, but a significant strand sees language as first and foremost social, before it is about giving information or instructions. We are social animals because we can speak, and we speak because we desire to communicate, to have fellowship with others.

In this reading, the apostle Paul uses the metaphor of clothing to explore what social life looks like in Christian communities. We are to wear Christ as the 'outward vesture' and 'inner clothing' of our lives. Paul describes a beautiful Jesus-like outfit of kindness, humility and love in direct contrast to a list of grim garments in the previous verses (3:5–9). It's as if Paul is holding up before us two different wardrobes, two very different kinds of social lives.

And how do we speak to one another in Christian community? Paul says that the word of Christ ('the King's speech') is our communal language. We grow together as we apply Jesus' message to every aspect of our lives in ongoing conversations. And together we are to sing songs giving thanks to God. After all, if singing is the most original and social form of language, as some suggest, that's another sign we are made above all for communion with our creator God and harmony with others.

> 'Let holy charity mine outward vesture be and lowliness become mine inner clothing' (Bianco da Siena, 1350–99).

Matthew Prior

# Keeping the peace

## 1 Thessalonians 5:12–19

Dear brothers and sisters, honour those who are your leaders in the Lord's work. They work hard among you and give you spiritual guidance. Show them great respect and wholehearted love because of their work. And live peacefully with each other. Brothers and sisters, we urge you to warn those who are lazy. Encourage those who are timid. Take tender care of those who are weak. Be patient with everyone. See that no one pays back evil for evil, but always try to do good to each other and to all people. Always be joyful. Never stop praying. Be thankful in all circumstances, for this is God's will for you who belong to Christ Jesus. Do not stifle the Holy Spirit. (NLT)

### Reflection

What do we do with these end sections of Paul's letters that read like scattered thoughts, darting in different directions? Perhaps in his mind's eye, the apostle is lovingly scanning the church community, dispensing some choice but heartfelt closing words.

Different groups come into his sights in today's reading. Leaders, first of all, are commended to the whole church for their hard work. But then Paul tackles what is disturbing the peace of the Thessalonian fellowship.

Some lazy community members were causing disruption by refusing to earn a living (see 4:11), perhaps because they were more concerned with finding a patron than finding work. This is not just their problem; it's a community problem – and so the church is to take responsibility for steering them back towards worthwhile work. Similarly, the church is to take patient responsibility for the timid and the weak, who risked being confused with those who were wilfully shirking.

Other Christian community-killers, to judge from Paul's next few imperatives, are revenge, stifled joy, limited prayer and a complaining spirit towards God and one another. The last instruction is not to say we paste a smile over a hurting heart. As a wise church leader once told me, we can give thanks *in* all circumstances, even if we can't give thanks *for* all circumstances. To keep faith and thanks towards God in hard times is truly a gift of the Holy Spirit. And only a leader who has lived it, like the apostle Paul, can truly commend this gift to others.

Why not drop a note of encouragement to a church leader you value?

| Matthew Prior

# Fuller fellowship

## Hebrews 13:1–5, 7–8

> Let mutual love continue. Do not neglect to show hospitality to strangers, for by doing that some have entertained angels without knowing it. Remember those who are in prison, as though you were in prison with them; those who are being tortured, as though you yourselves were being tortured. Let marriage be held in honour by all, and let the marriage bed be kept undefiled; for God will judge fornicators and adulterers. Keep your lives free from the love of money, and be content with what you have... Remember your leaders, those who spoke the word of God to you; consider the outcome of their way of life, and imitate their faith. Jesus Christ is the same yesterday and today and forever. (NRSV)

| Matthew Prior

**Reflection**

A church near where I live has a thriving coffee shop called the He-Brews Café. Apart from having a great biblical name, it provides a daily hub for local community life. And operating a 'pay as you may' policy means that hospitality is at its heart.

'Fellowship' without the instruction in today's reading from Hebrews to welcome the stranger and empathise with those who are suffering has sometimes led to a church concerned with its own matters. When I was growing up, we lived near a local church 'fellowship' which was a tight-knit family of believers whose 'mutual love' seemed reserved for one another only. Eventually, this group opened up to sharing fellowship with other Christians, but it took their godly church leader to play a key role in encouraging unity with other believers and the transformation of their local community.

As well as advocating hospitable fellowship, the writer of this letter is clear that faithful teaching matters hugely, not least in sexual ethics. Church leaders are portrayed as role models, against the wonderful background of the creedal phrase 'Jesus Christ is the same yesterday and today and forever.' The incarnate Lord is for all time our ultimate standard, and perhaps we hear in this passage echoes of his remarkable teaching about welcoming strangers and visiting prisoners: 'Truly I tell you, whatever you did for one of the least of these brothers and sisters of mine, you did for me' (Matthew 25:40, NIV).

To whom and how can you show hospitality today?

| Matthew Prior

# The things we love

## James 2:1–5 (abridged)

My dear brothers and sisters, how can you claim to have faith in our glorious Lord Jesus Christ if you favour some people over others? For example, suppose someone comes into your meeting dressed in fancy clothes and expensive jewelry, and another comes in who is poor and dressed in dirty clothes. If you give special attention and a good seat to the rich person, but you say to the poor one, 'You can stand over there, or else sit on the floor' – well, doesn't this discrimination show that your judgements are guided by evil motives?... Hasn't God chosen the poor in this world to be rich in faith? Aren't they the ones who will inherit the Kingdom he promised to those who love him?

(NLT)

**Reflection**

We'd like to think that we're no longer prone to the blatant bias to the rich singled out by James in this reading. After all, in the ancient world, getting on the right side of a wealthy patron seemed to many to be the best route to survival. But surely, our society now strives for equality, the heir of Christian values, and many churches seem convinced of a 'bias to the poor'. Aren't Christians now more likely to be inverse-snobs than sycophants to the rich?

My twelve-year-old is impressed by shiny fast cars. I grew out of that a while ago, but I must confess, if I'm honest, that I'm still rather wowed in the presence of a rich and impressive person. How did they make it? And the seemingly noble thought pops into my head: wouldn't it be good to have them 'onside'? Think of the good we could do. As one wealthy businessman once told a church leader I know, 'If I tithed, you wouldn't know what to do with it!'

James doesn't mince his words: don't be wowed by wealth. After all, the things we love determine the kind of community we live in. A community in love with money doesn't truly love God or his people. God's kingdom community is his ultimate gift to the people who love him above all else.

Take a quiet moment to ask the Holy Spirit to shine a light on any ways you might be 'wowed by wealth'. And pray for someone you know under the spell of money, either their own or someone else's.

| Matthew Prior

# Saving faith

## James 2:14–18

What good is it, dear brothers and sisters, if you say you have faith but don't show it by your actions? Can that kind of faith save anyone? Suppose you see a brother or sister who has no food or clothing, and you say, 'Good-bye and have a good day; stay warm and eat well' – but then you don't give that person any food or clothing. What good does that do? So you see, faith by itself isn't enough. Unless it produces good deeds, it is dead and useless. Now someone may argue, 'Some people have faith; others have good deeds.' But I say, 'How can you show me your faith if you don't have good deeds? I will show you my faith by my good deeds.' (NLT)

| Matthew Prior

Reflection

Martin Luther famously criticised James as a 'letter of straw', opposed, he thought, to the clarity of Paul's gospel of justification by faith (Galatians 2:16). But James is not commending good deeds as a means of earning salvation. With Paul, in fact, James agrees that faith spells love and that 'the only thing that counts is faith expressing itself through love' (Galatians 5:66, NIV).

Overcoming the opposition of faith and social action may seem to be a dead issue for the UK church today. Surely we've got this by now! But think again, for there is something insidious and ever-present about our tendency to find justification in what we're instinctively drawn to – whether that is personal spirituality or practical action.

And the tragic thing is that if we separate one from the other, we will kill what we think we value. Spiritual life without loving works all too easily becomes overblown and disconnected from reality – lifeless, as James says. Works without living faith all too easily becomes overbearing and insensitive to people's real needs – self-defeating.

The work of Church Action on Poverty (CAP) is a recent shining example of faith expressing itself in love. One CAP worker who left a settled career to work alongside the UK's poorest told me, 'I got tired of a career of making rich people even richer… my life had to count for something more.'

> What one action will you do as a result of reading this passage today? How can your faith express itself in practical love, extending the reach of fellowship?

# Transforming conflict

## 1 Peter 3:8–11

Finally, all of you should be of one mind. Sympathise with each other. Love each other as brothers and sisters. Be tenderhearted, and keep a humble attitude. Don't repay evil for evil. Don't retaliate with insults when people insult you. Instead, pay them back with a blessing. That is what God has called you to do, and he will grant you his blessing. For the Scriptures say, 'If you want to enjoy life and see many happy days, keep your tongue from speaking evil and your lips from telling lies. Turn away from evil and do good. Search for peace, and work to maintain it.'

(NLT)

### Reflection

The happiness movement has taken off in recent years, with churches offering Happiness Labs and Happiness Courses. These initiatives are surfing a wave of science of well-being, which has set out to address 'Affluenza', psychologist Oliver James' memorable diagnosis for the general malaise in consumerist societies caused by always wanting what other people (seem to) have. The happiness movement has huge potential, as it asks what truly makes us happy.

The instructions in this reading from 1 Peter, drawing on Psalm 34, give a frank response. It starts with the assumption that Christians have a radically distinctive way of understanding ourselves and relating to others. The attributes listed in verse 8 are about our mindset. Being 'of one mind' suggests not agreement on every little detail but a community where people basically want the same thing: to know God more. And having 'a humble mind' implies we have no illusions about our weakness and our dependence on God for life and for forgiveness.

Wanting the same thing and being humble does not mean that conflict is abnormal for Christians. Conflict is 'difference plus tension' and it's inevitable – that's why these words were written in the first place! What matters is whether we can transform conflict as we dig into a common desire for more of God and a basic honesty about ourselves. Only that combination can truly make us happy, enabling us to receive God's peace and even pursue it beyond the walls of our church, physical and metaphorical, in a world that can sometimes be hostile to Christian faith.

> How can you search for peace today, especially with those who've hurt you?

# Multisensory fellowship

## 1 John 1:1–4

> We proclaim to you the one who existed from the beginning, whom we have heard and seen. We saw him with our own eyes and touched him with our own hands. He is the Word of life. This one who is life itself was revealed to us, and we have seen him. And now we testify and proclaim to you that he is the one who is eternal life. He was with the Father, and then he was revealed to us. We proclaim to you what we ourselves have actually seen and heard so that you may have fellowship with us. And our fellowship is with the Father and with his Son, Jesus Christ. We are writing these things so that you may fully share our joy. (NLT)

**Reflection**

As I write this, it's almost Christmas and there's perhaps no better reading than this passage to express the meaning of Christmas. Here we soar to the heights of eternity and enter into the intimacy of fellowship, or communion, with the God who is from the beginning. But we also stay rooted in visible, audible, tangible reality, because the life of God was revealed in an ordinary yet extraordinary human life, lived by a man named Jesus in a real time and place, among real people.

Yet those closest to the human-divine Son do not want this ultimate gift to be lost in history. Rather they want to regift it, so that the joy of knowing not just the Son but also the Father who sent him, and the joy of knowing others as fellow children of God, can be widely shared. So John writes to regift the eternal gift that doesn't diminish when shared, but also to head off those who are hawking a cheap and nasty imitation. The identity of John's competitors (so-called Gnostics) can only be pieced together, but they seemed to prefer an ethereal 'Christ spirituality' to the intellectually and ethically demanding message of a God who became flesh.

Does this debate still matter today? Absolutely! Ethereal (unearthly) spirituality will always be more appealing than truly incarnational (down-to-earth) faith, which is as intellectually and ethically demanding as it ever was. But only the truth can satisfy us and set us free.

> How can you worship God with your body at Christmas
> (or the next upcoming festival)?

**FELLOWSHIP**

# Real love

## 1 John 3:14–18

If we love our brothers and sisters who are believers, it proves that we have passed from death to life. But a person who has no love is still dead. Anyone who hates another brother or sister is really a murderer at heart. And you know that murderers don't have eternal life within them. We know what real love is because Jesus gave up his life for us. So we also ought to give up our lives for our brothers and sisters. If someone has enough money to live well and sees a brother or sister in need but shows no compassion – how can God's love be in that person? Dear children, let's not merely say that we love each other; let us show the truth by our actions. (NLT)

**Reflection**

'What is love?', 'Where is love?', 'Is this love?', 'How deep is your love?'

I could go on, but you get the picture, or the lyric, in this case. Love is an eternal question in human culture, high and low, the deepest of mysteries. The first letter of John starts from the assumption that human beings don't know true love until it's revealed to us. And it suggests, too, that human beings generally prefer to talk about love than to put love in action.

To say this is not to assume that Christians (or Christian writers) have the moral high ground. According to John, defining what love is and is not can never be a comfortable activity kept for the lecture room. Love is a battleground, where death and life, hatred, murder and sacrifice are the order of the day. John knows too that those who claim to follow Christ are just as prone to dislike, even to hate, others, despite the pretty words we use.

Since the fall (1 John 3:12 references Cain), there has been a battle raging across human history and within every single human life – will I show love in action or merely in words? And the wonderful news we find here is that, for all time, the mystery of love has been unveiled and the ultimate battle for our hearts has been won, 'because Jesus gave up his life for us'.

How will you enter into Jesus' victory today, by showing God's love in action at work, at home, at church?

| Matthew Prior

# Keeping it real

## 1 John 4:7–12

Dear friends, let us continue to love one another, for love comes from God. Anyone who loves is a child of God and knows God. But anyone who does not love does not know God, for God is love. God showed how much he loved us by sending his one and only Son into the world so that we might have eternal life through him. This is real love – not that we loved God, but that he loved us and sent his Son as a sacrifice to take away our sins. Dear friends, since God loved us that much, we surely ought to love each other. No one has ever seen God. But if we love each other, God lives in us, and his love is brought to full expression in us. (NLT)

### Reflection

'No one has ever seen God.' How can John say this, given his insistence on the multisensory revelation of God's Word in a human life (1 John 1:1)? To understand why John is so careful is not an academic exercise; it keeps our faith rooted in its Jewish soil and makes us fruitful lovers.

The Old Testament insists that the true God is not a mental projection or a reflection of the best of us. The eternal and ever-loving God is beyond compare, strictly unimaginable for us. We do not naturally know love or recognise real love. So John does not tell us that love is God, or that whatever we call love makes God present in the world. No, he tells us that the unseen God, who is beyond our wildest dreams, can be revealed only when he makes our lives his home, as he did first and foremost in the life of Jesus. And Jesus didn't just show us a love that we all know already; he defines love and makes it possible for us too.

So let's get practical. Who are you tempted to stop loving at the moment? Is it a close family member, a spouse or a parent? A work colleague? Someone from church who has hurt you? Loving that person does not mean that we have no boundaries, but it means we cannot refuse the duty to love.

> Pray that you might regift God's love to someone today.

FELLOWSHIP

# Home at last

## Revelation 21:1–5 (abridged)

Then I saw a new heaven and a new earth; for the first heaven and the first earth had passed away, and the sea was no more. And I saw the holy city, the new Jerusalem, coming down out of heaven from God, prepared as a bride adorned for her husband. And I heard a loud voice from the throne saying, 'See, the home of God is among mortals. He will dwell with them; they will be his peoples, and God himself will be with them; he will wipe every tear from their eyes. Death will be no more; mourning and crying and pain will be no more, for the first things have passed away.' And the one who was seated on the throne said, 'See, I am making all things new.' (NRSV)

| Matthew Prior

### Reflection

Nothing will ever be the same again! There are moments on the grand canvas of history and in the intimate weaving of our lives when something new comes from God to us. And when that happens, it's because the promise revealed in this passage, of God dwelling with us, is breaking in now. If we receive a foretaste of the promise, it's because one day we will know its fullness: a total final transformation of all things. Yet here, the cosmic and the intimate belong together, for what comes first is a renewed fellowship between God and us: 'See, the home of God is among mortals. He will dwell with them.'

Our estrangement from God will be overcome, as what the incarnation began in the time of human history will be fulfilled at its end. This is truly fellowship because God is *with us* without overpowering us. We are not absorbed into God: God is fully God and we are now fully human – in all our glorious diversity (note the plural reference to 'peoples' here). What is eliminated is all that ruins this creation, with death, the ultimate enemy, defeated.

Still, we are not yet at the end, so to complete these readings, can I ask you to reflect on your present experience: how will you anticipate this promise today?

> How can the promise that you will live forever in God's immediate presence renew your intimacy with God today?

# Whole-church resources

MISSIONAL DISCIPLESHIP RESOURCES FOR CHURCHES

Individual copy £4.99

Holy Habits is an adventure in Christian discipleship. Inspired by Luke's model of church found in Acts 2:42–47, it identifies ten habits and encourages the development of a way of life formed by them. These resources are designed to help churches explore the habits creatively in a range of contexts and live them out in whole-life, intergenerational, missional discipleship.

# HOLYHABITS

Original design by morsebrowndesign.co.uk & penguinbox

# Group Studies

Edited by Andrew Roberts
Individual copy  £6.99

These new additions to the Holy Habits resources have been developed to help church groups explore the Holy Habits through prayerful engagement with the Bible and live them out in whole-life, missional discipleship.

Each leader's guide contains eight sessions of Bible study material, providing off-the-peg material to help churches get started or continue with Holy Habits. Each session includes a Bible passage, reflection, group questions, community/outreach ideas, art and media links and a prayer.

Other Bible Reflections currently available:

Edited by Andrew Roberts
Individual copy  £3.99

Group Studies and Bible Reflections for the remaining five habits
BREAKING BREAD | SHARING RESOURCES | SERVING | GLADNESS AND GENEROSITY | WORSHIP will be available in February 2020.

Find out more at holyhabits.org.uk
and brfonline.org.uk/collections/holy-habits
Download a leaflet for your church leadership at
brfonline.org.uk/holyhabitsdownload

# Are you looking to continue the habit of daily Bible reading?

With a subscription to BRF Bible reading notes, you'll have everything you need to nourish your relationship with the Bible and with God.

Our most popular and longest running series, *New Daylight*, features daily readings and reflections from a selection of much-beloved writers, dealing with a variety of themes and Bible passages. With the relevant passage printed alongside the comment, *New Daylight* is a practical and effective way of reading the Bible as a part of your everyday routine.

*New Daylight* is available in print, deluxe (large print), by email and as an app for iOS and Android.

'I think Bible reading notes are really underrated. At any age – there I was as a teenager getting as much out of them then as I am now – so they're for every age group, not just the very young and the very old. I think to have them as your bedside companion is a really wise idea throughout life.'

Debbie Thrower, Pioneer of BRF's Anna Chaplaincy programme

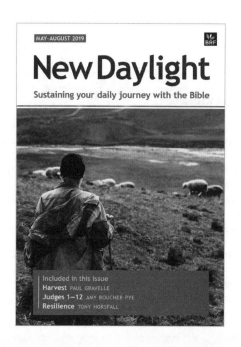

MAY–AUGUST 2019

BRF

# New Daylight

Sustaining your daily journey with the Bible

Included in this issue
**Harvest** PAUL GRAVELLE
**Judges 1—12** AMY BOUCHER PYE
**Resilience** TONY HORSFALL

Also available:

  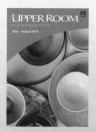 

Find out more at brfonline.org.uk

# Praise for the original Holy Habits resources

'Here are some varied and rich resources to help further deepen our discipleship of Christ, encouraging and enabling us to adopt the life-transforming habits that make for following Jesus.'
Revd Dr Martyn Atkins, Team Leader & Superintendent Minister, Methodist Central Hall, Westminster

'The Holy Habits resources will help you, your church, your fellowship group, to engage in a journey of discovery about what it really means to be a disciple today. I know you will be encouraged, challenged and inspired as you read and work your way through… There is lots to study together and pray about, and that can only be good as our churches today seek to bring about the kingdom of God.'
Revd Loraine Mellor, President of the Methodist Conference 2017/18

'The Holy Habits resources help weave the spiritual through everyday life. They're a great tool that just get better with use. They help us grow in our desire to follow Jesus as their concern is formation not simply information.'
Olive Fleming Drane and John Drane

'The Holy Habits resources are an insightful and comprehensive manual for living in the way of Jesus in the 21st century: an imaginative, faithful and practical gift for the church that will sustain and invigorate our life and mission in a demanding world. The Holy Habits resources are potentially transformational for a church.'
Revd Ian Adams, Mission Spirituality Adviser for Church Mission Society

'To understand the disciplines of the Christian life without practising them habitually is like owning a fine collection of soap but never having a wash. The team behind Holy Habits knows this, which is why they have produced these excellent and practical resources. Use them, and by God's grace you will grow in holiness.'
Paul Bayes, Bishop of Liverpool